THIS OLD CAR
A COUNTING BOOK

THIS OLD CAR
A COUNTING BOOK

COLIN
AND
JACQUI
HAWKINS

ORCHARD BOOKS
London

Text and illustrations copyright © Colin and Jacqui Hawkins 1988
First published in Great Britain in 1988 by
ORCHARD BOOKS
10 Golden Square, London W1R 3AF
Orchard Books Australia
14 Mars Road, Lane Cove NSW 2066
Orchard Books Canada
20 Torbay Road, Markham, Ontario 23P 1G6
1 85213 018 0
Typeset in Great Britain by Tradespools Limited, Frome, Somerset
Printed in Belgium by Proost

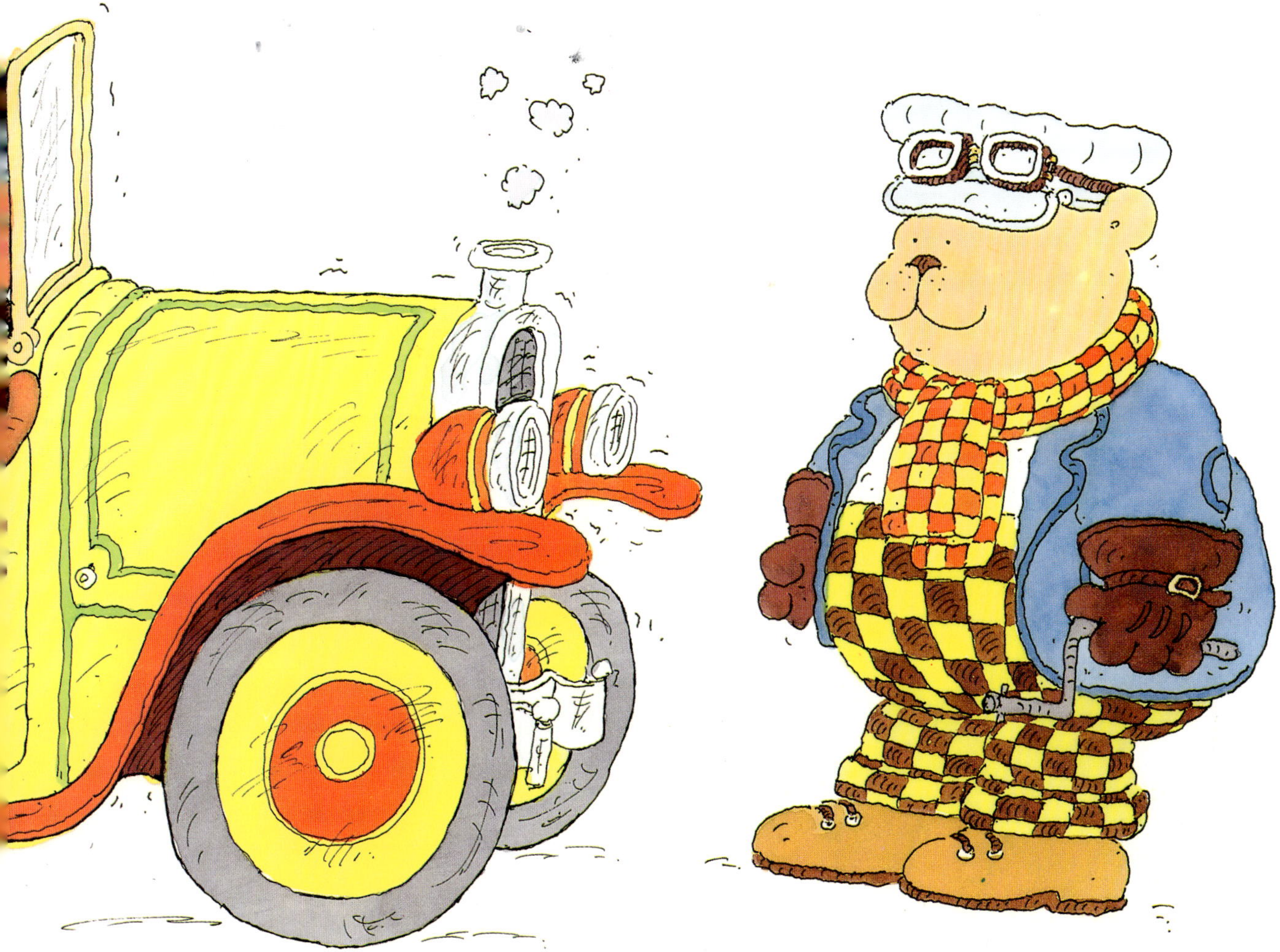

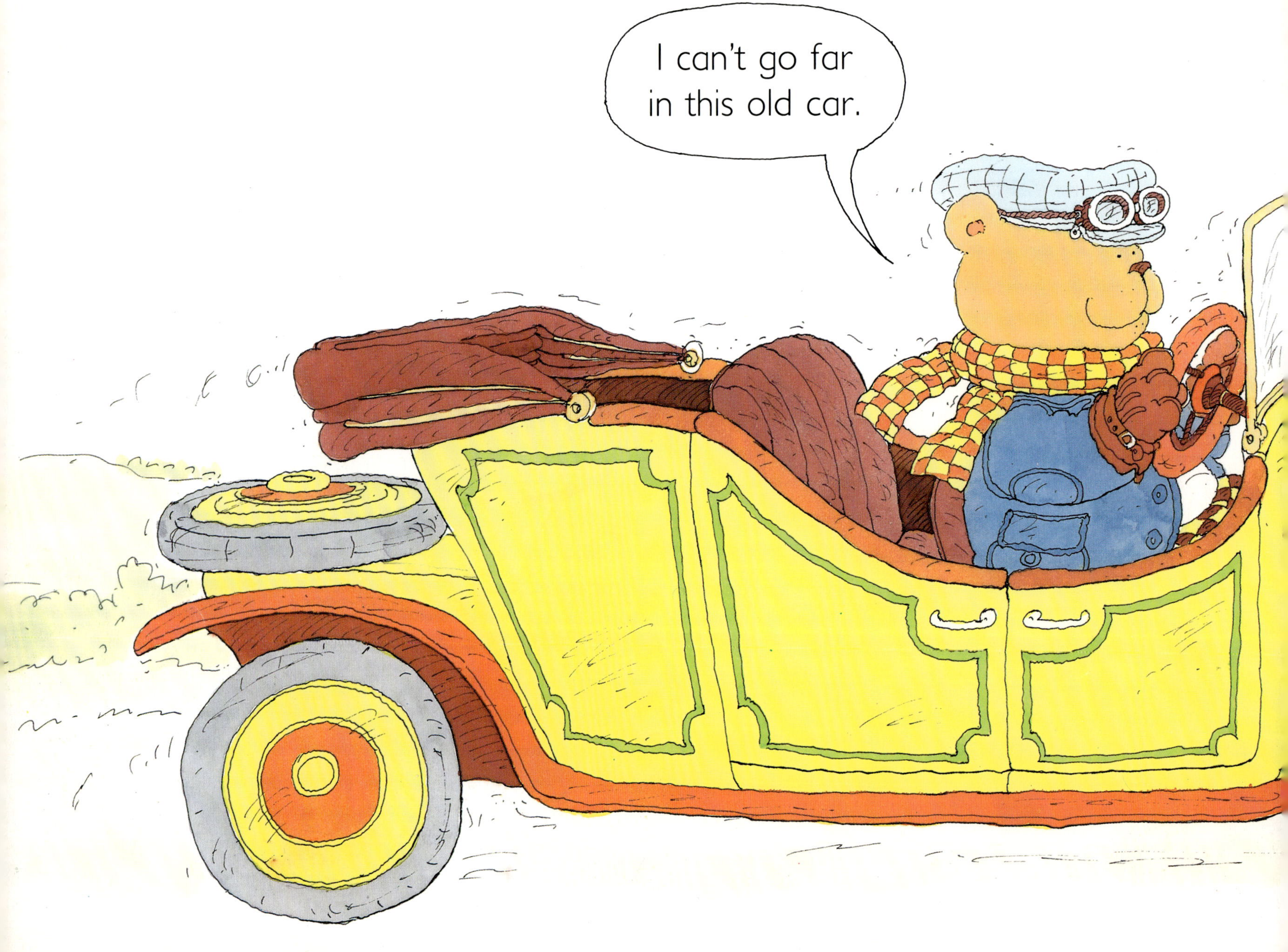
I can't go far in this old car.

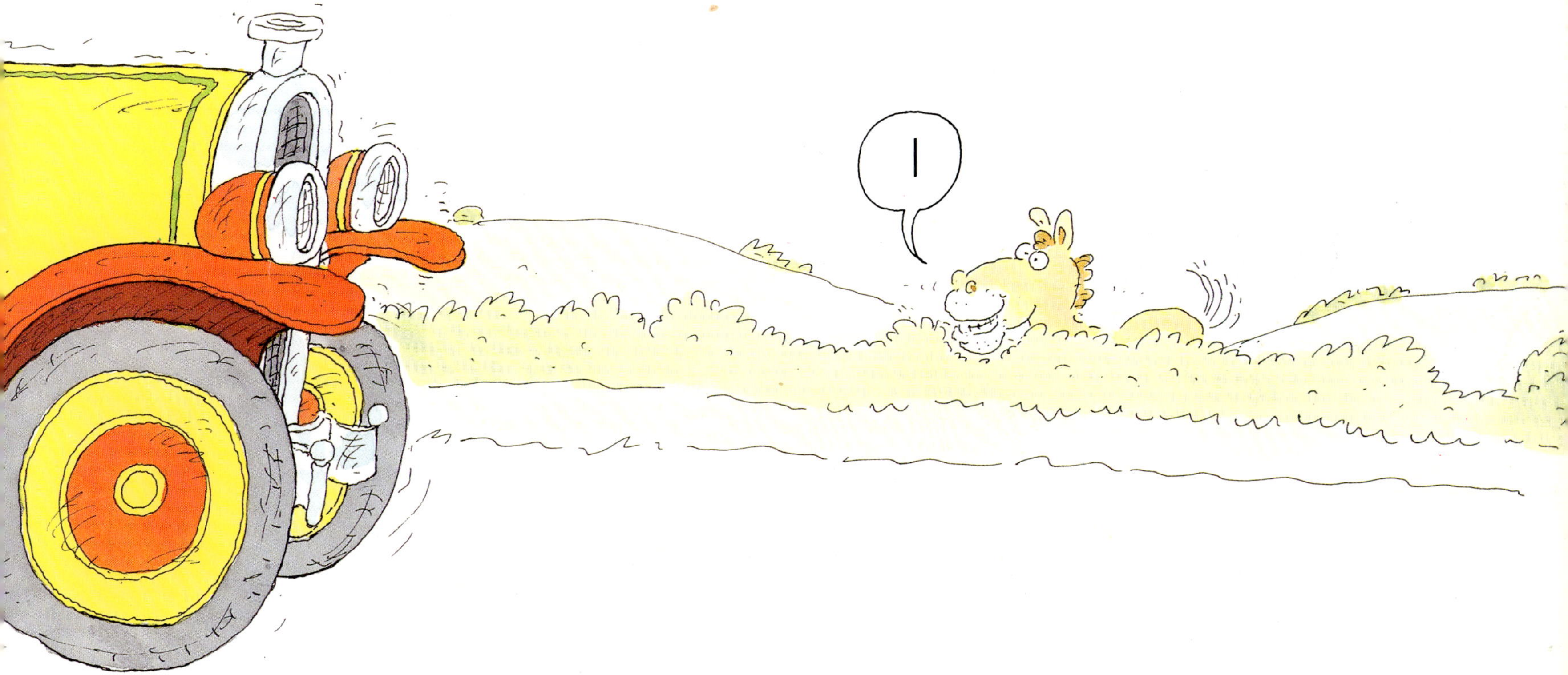
I

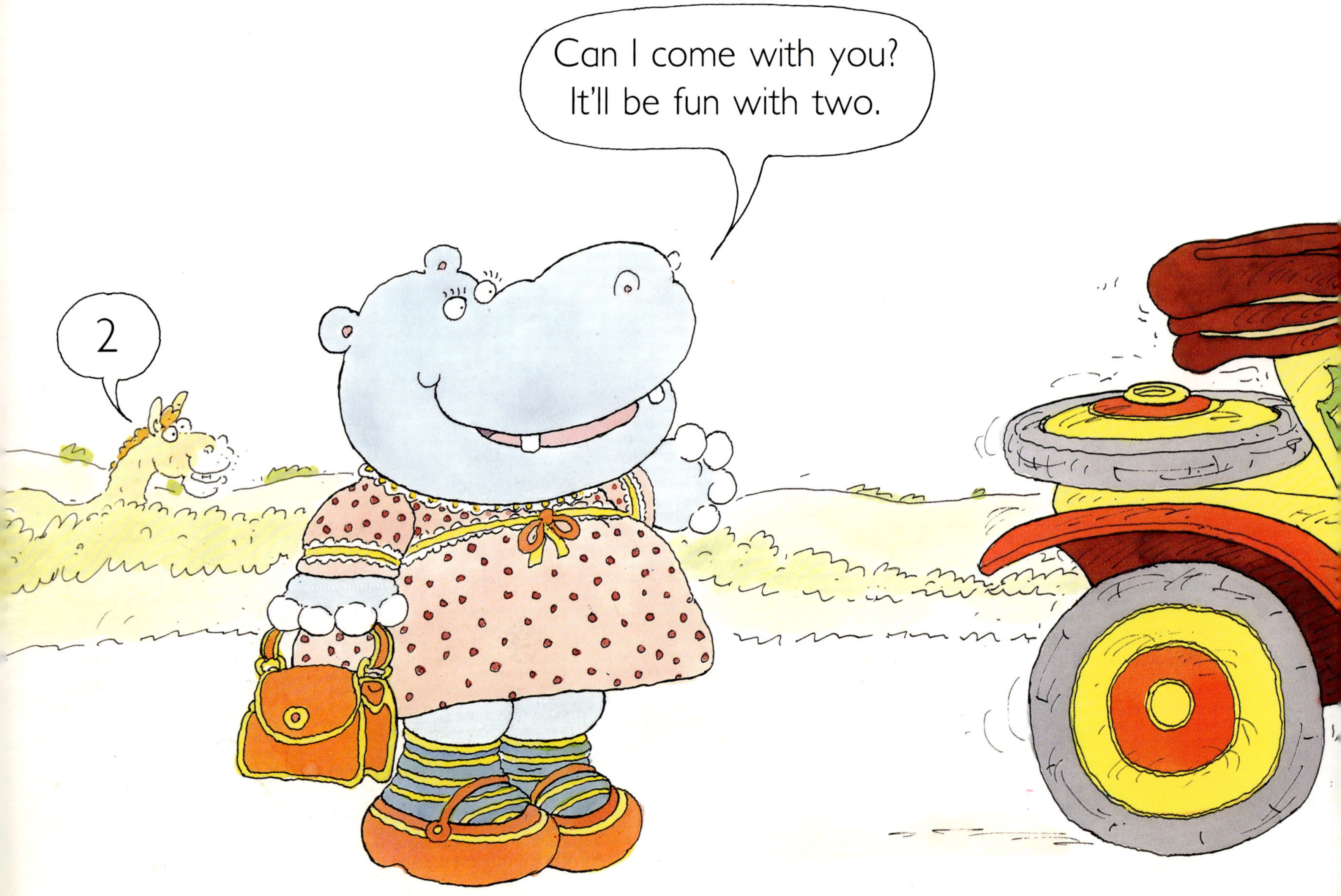
Can I come with you?
It'll be fun with two.
2

This car is not strong, I've had it too long.

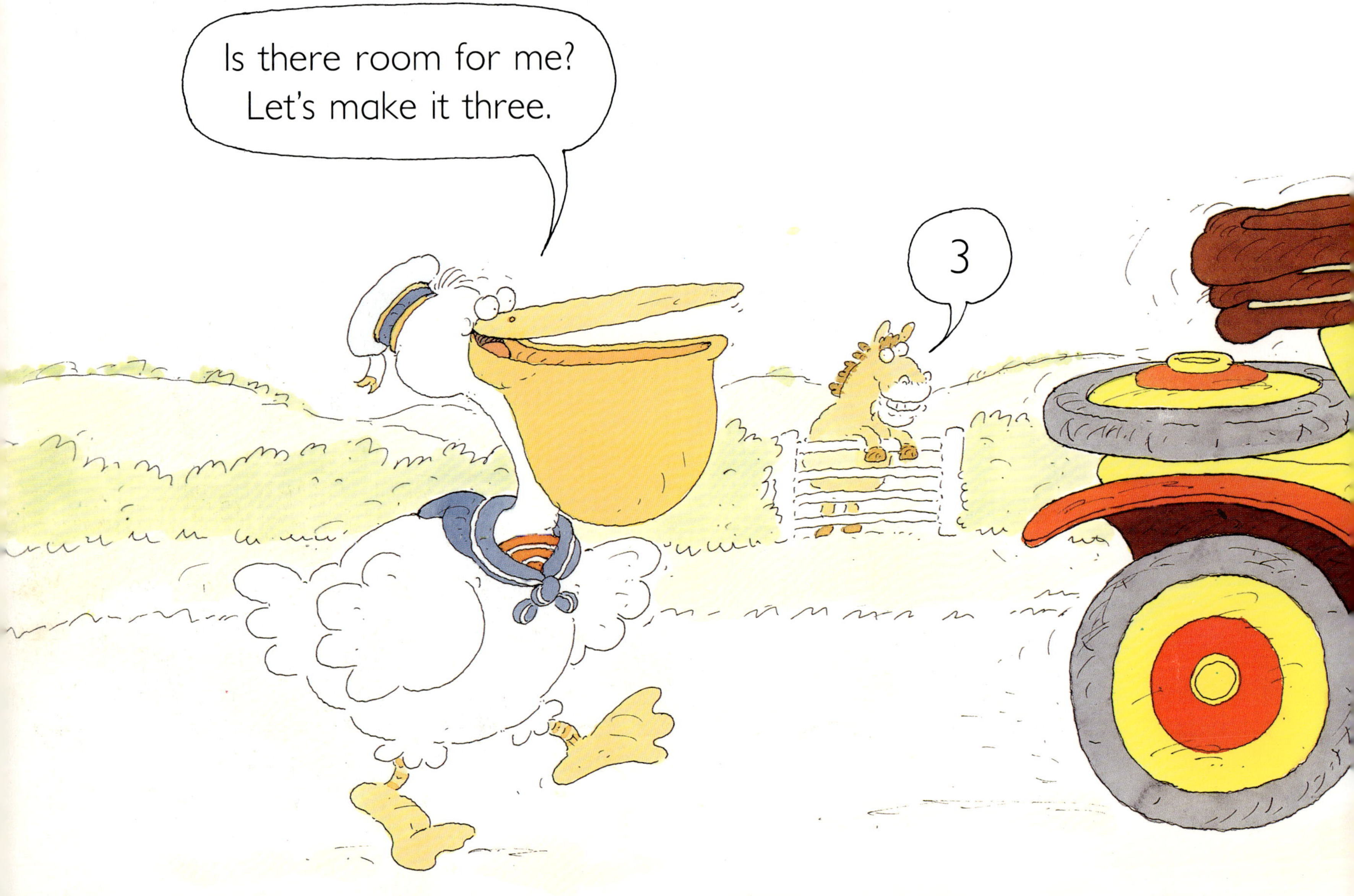
Is there room for me?
Let's make it three.
3

"What a cheek!
Just look at that beak!"

"How much more can it take?
Do you want it to break?"

"There's room for one more, it will only make four."

4

Give us a smile, Crocodile.
Good grief! What big teeth!
Well, just for a mile, Crocodile.

"Can I come for a drive? It will only make five."

"Go for a run, you'll have more fun."

5

What a twit,
where will he fit?
I'd like to please,
but where will you squeeze?

"What a wonderful mix! Let's make it six."

"What a big lump, give her a thump."

6

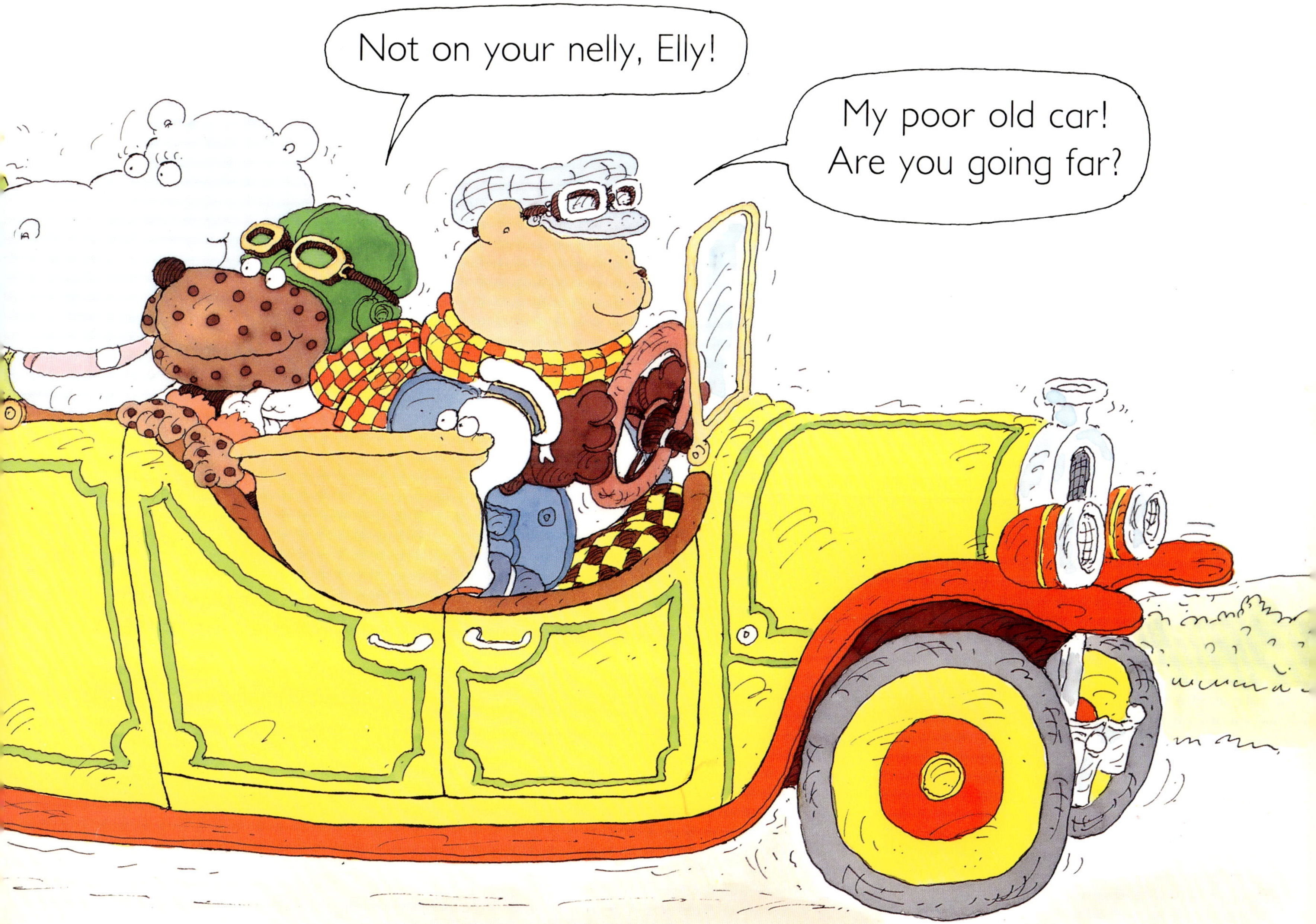
Not on your nelly, Elly!
My poor old car! Are you going far?

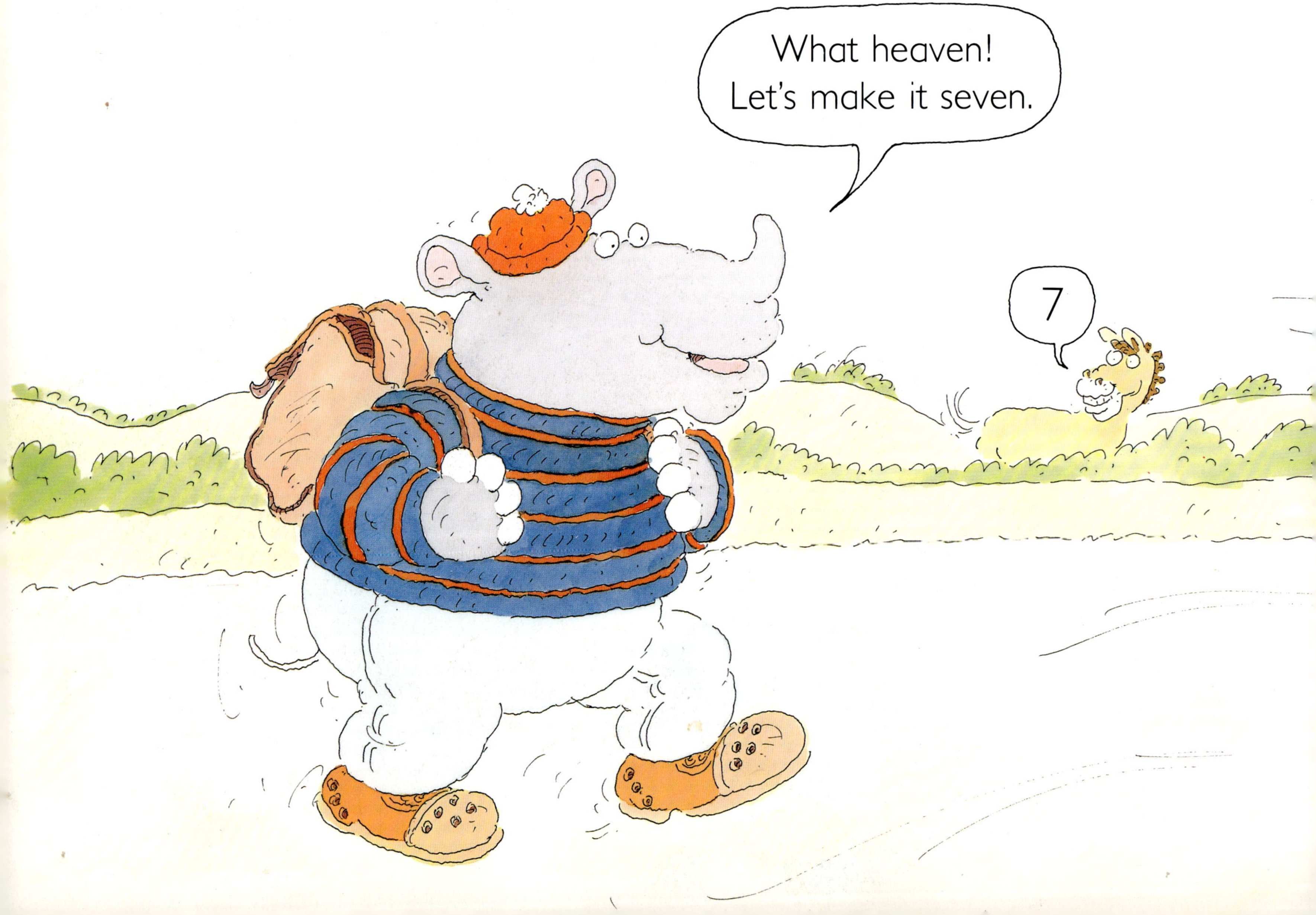
What heaven! Let's make it seven.
7

What a nerve, he made you swerve.
Wouldn't you know, here comes Rhino.
Don't open the door, he'll go through the floor

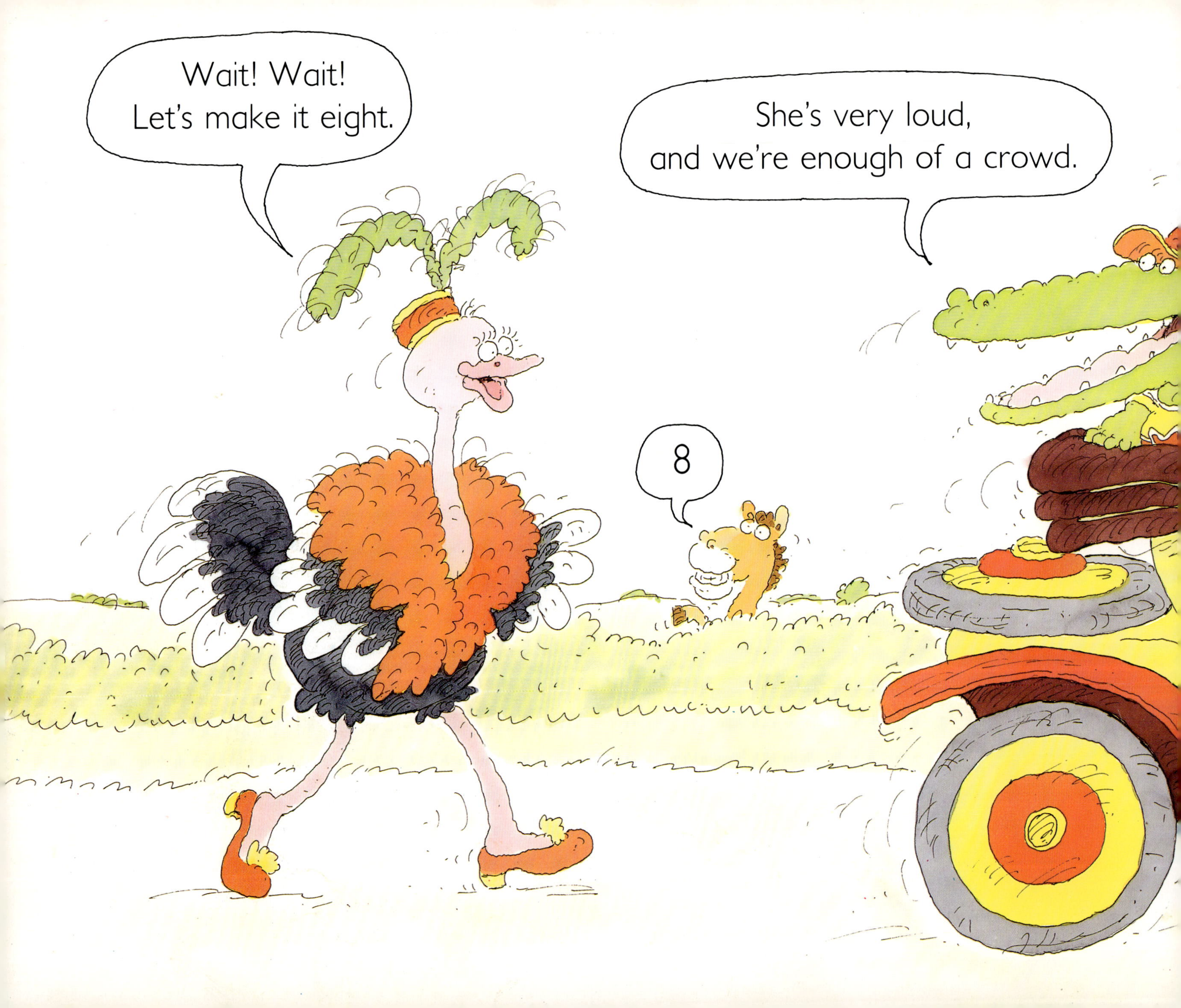
Wait! Wait!
Let's make it eight.
She's very loud,
and we're enough of a crowd.
8

There's enough of us. Get a bus.
I'm going to be late, and my car's in a state!

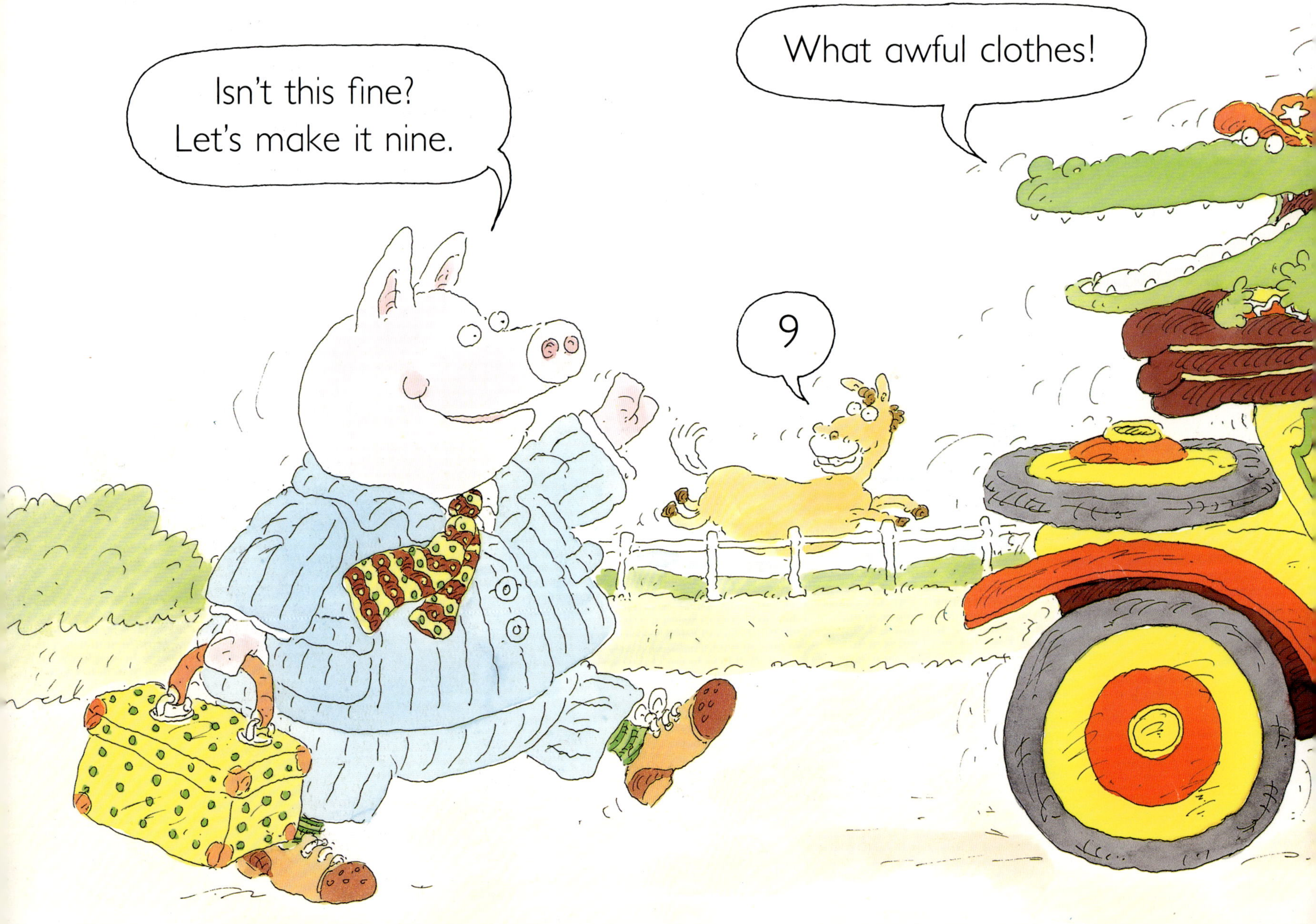
Isn't this fine?
Let's make it nine.
9
What awful clothes!

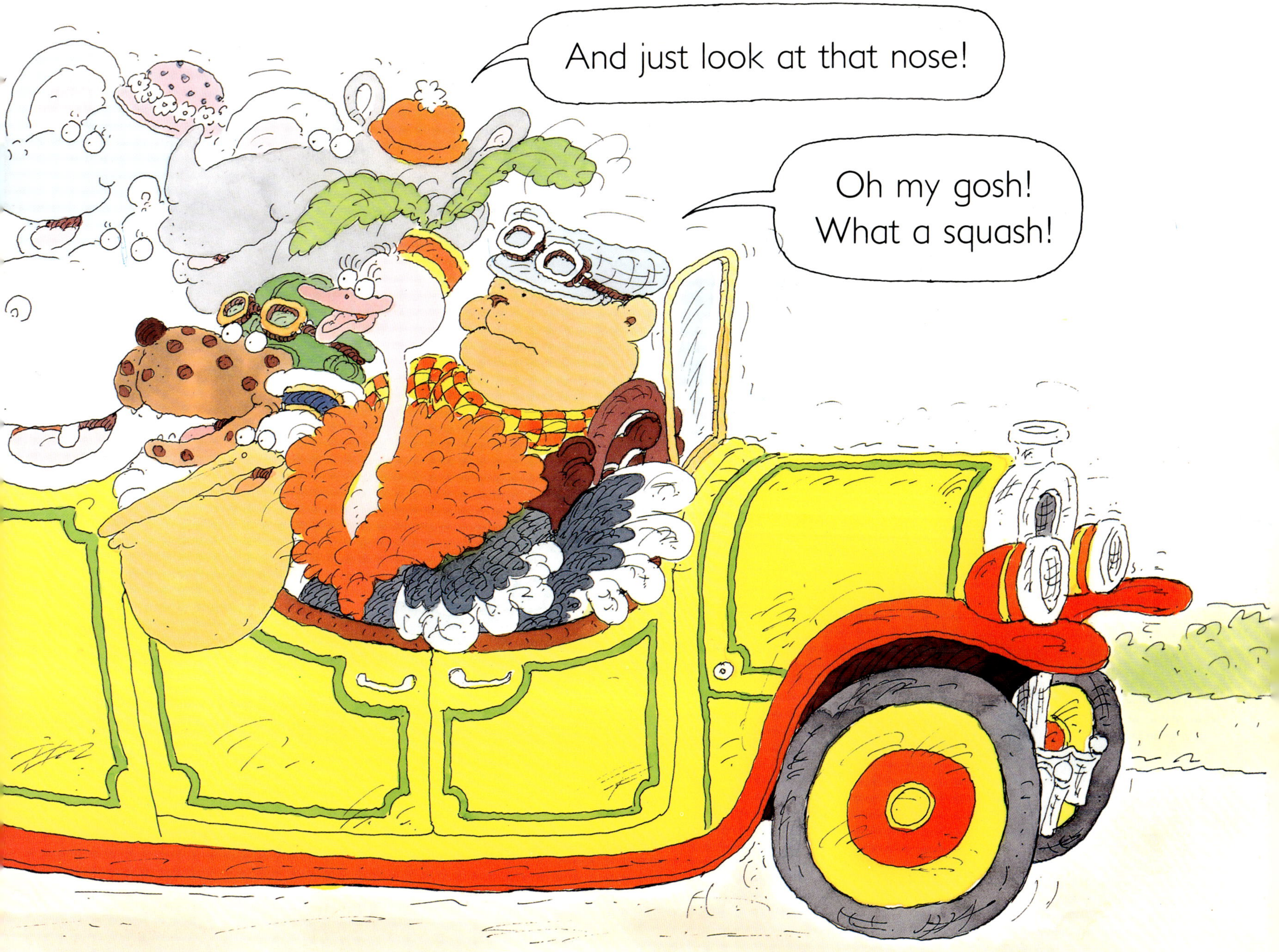
And just look at that nose!
Oh my gosh! What a squash!

"He'll wriggle and squirm like a big worm."

"It's a big mistake to take that snake."

"Come on, then! Let'sssssssss make it ten!"

10

"Well, if he wriggles about, we'll all fall out!"

"My car will break with that fat snake."

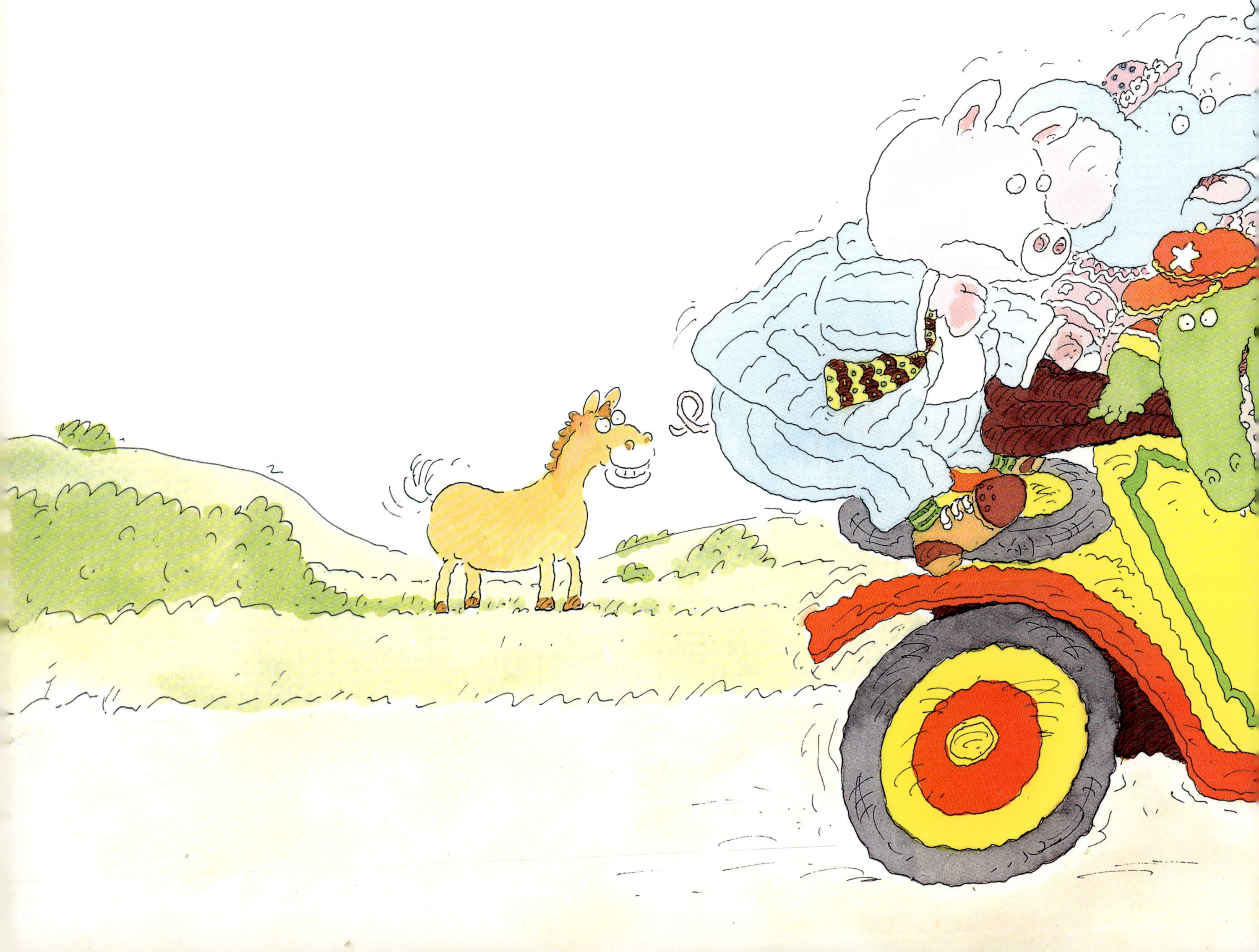

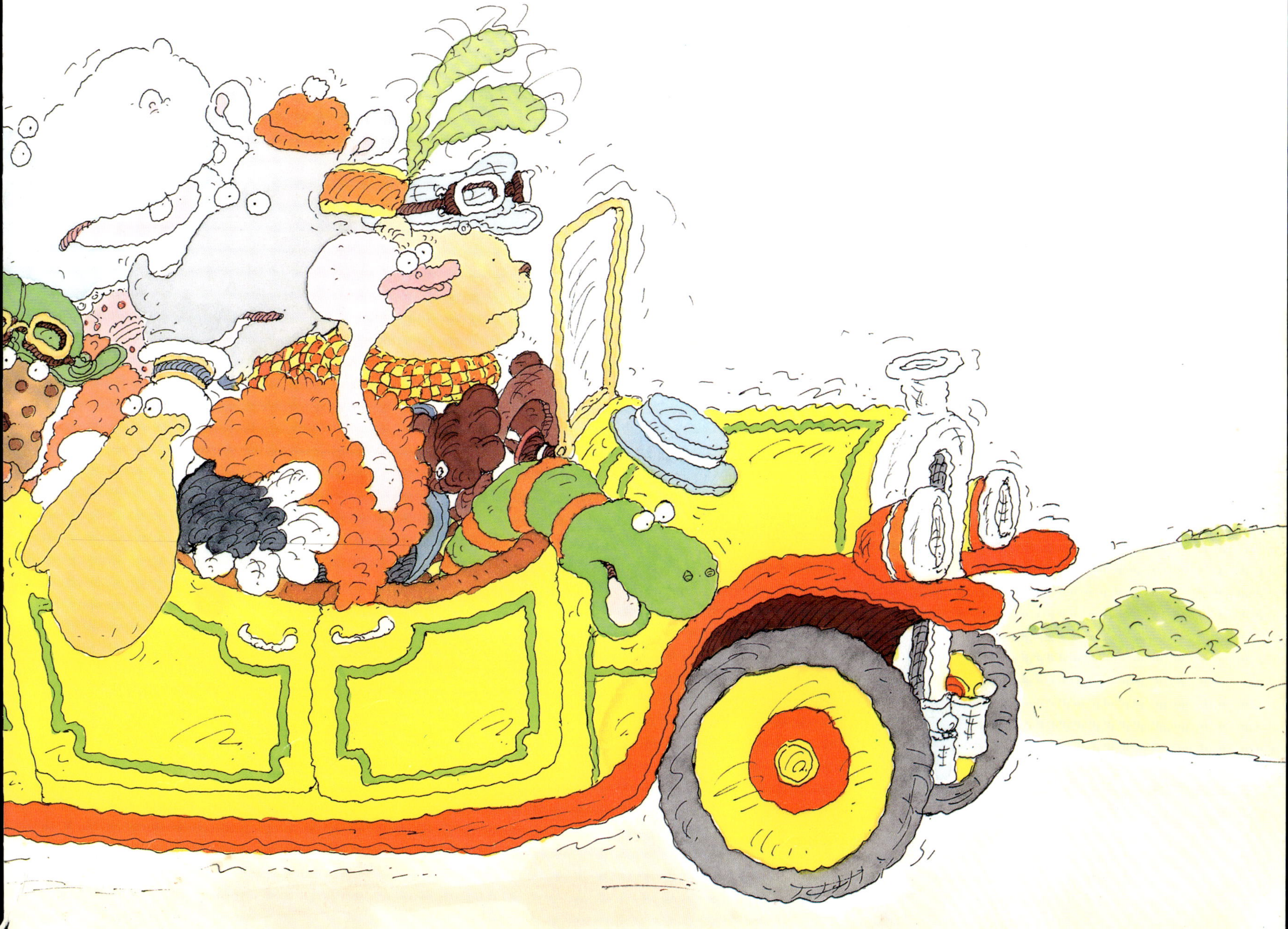

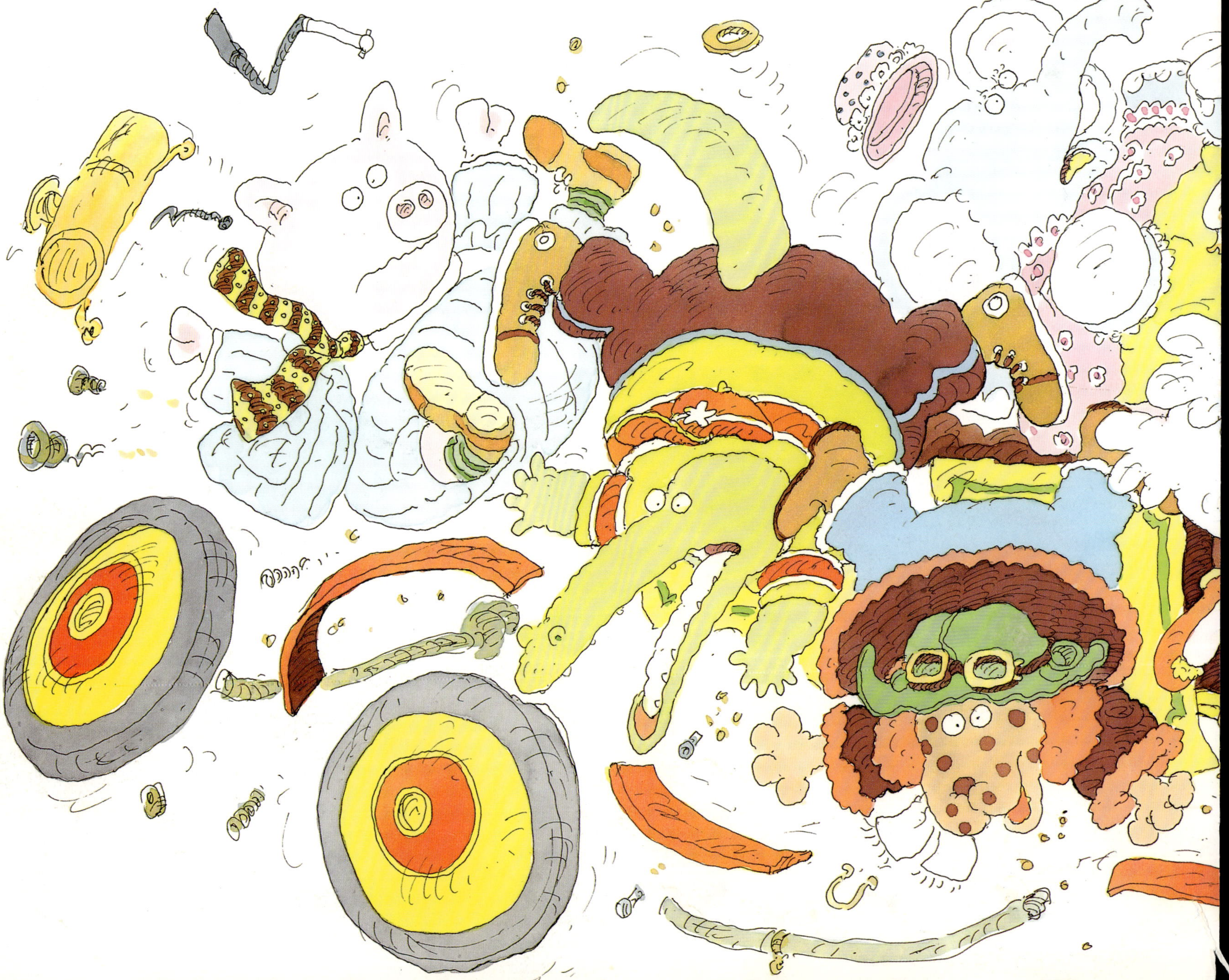

BANG!

"Look what you've done! It should have been one."

"But with me and you it only made two."

"Then with me it only made three."

"With just one more it only made four."

"It was a great drive when there were five."

"It was such a good mix when there were six."

"It was heaven when there were seven."

"It was really great when there were eight."

"I thought it was fine. We only made nine."

"Wassssss it too many then, when we were ten?"

PRINTED IN BELGIUM BY
proost
INTERNATIONAL BOOK PRODUCTION